The Hum of it All

Poems from a Personal Journey

Eugene C. Bianchi

The Hum of it All: Poems from a Personal Journey
ISBN: Softcover 978-1-946478-15-3
Copyright © 2017 by Eugene C. Bianchi

All rights reserved. No part of this book may be reproduced or transmitted in any form or by any means, electronic or mechanical, including photocopying, recording, or by any information storage and retrieval system, without permission in writing from the publisher.

To order additional copies of this book, contact:

Parson's Porch Books
1-423-475-7308
www.parsonsporch.com

Parson's Porch Books is an imprint of **Parson's Porch & Book Publishers** in Cleveland, Tennessee, which has double focus. We focus on the needs of creative writers who need a professional publisher to get their work to market, **&** we also focus on the needs of others by sharing our profits with those who struggle in poverty to meet their basic needs of food, clothing, shelter and safety.

Also by Eugene C. Bianchi

Chewing Down My Barn: Poems from the Carpenter Bees

Ear to the Ground: Poems from the Long View

Taking a Long Road Home: A Memoir

The Children's Crusade: Scandal at the Vatican

The Bishop of San Francisco: Romance, Intrigue and Religion

Elder Wisdom: Crafting Your Own Elderhood

On Growing Older

Aging as a Spiritual Journey

For more:

www.bianchibooks.com

Contents

INTRODUCTION	9
PRELUDE	11
A Nightingale of the Temescal*	13
BY THE OCONEE	15
Beauty and Depression	16
An Inward Olympics	17
Are We God(s)?	18
Bringing Earth to Heaven	19
Conversations with a Carolina Wren	20
Hawk and Dove at the River	22
Oak Leaves and a Puzzled Deer	23
Red Hawk Teaches Meditation	24
Reluctant Nectar Seekers	25
Spirit Gift	27
Listen to the Silence	28
Talking with a Spider	28
The Oconee is Agitated	30
The Owl and the Mockingbird	31
DEALING WITH CANCER	33
Cancer and Oneness	34
Beauty and Anxiety	35
Compassion and Ransom	36
Crow's Voice at MD Anderson Cancer Hospital	37
Martians and Earthlings	38
The Chair Undergirds Civilization	39
Here Comes Trouble	40
Varian, My Linear Accelerator	41
Belonging in Bishop's Park	42
CAT MAX MINISTRY	43
Cats for Reconciliation,	44
Death as Destiny not Defeat	45
Freedom Point	46
Spiritual Infrastructures on Election Night	47
The Hard and the Soft	48
The Hum of It All	49
The None Box	50
Be Lamps Unto Yourselves	51
REFLECTIONS ON RELIGION	53
Francis Dances America	54
General William Booth* and Senator Bernie Sanders Enter Heaven	55
Inner Doors of Perception	57
Insecurity in Wee Hours	58

Is Jesus God?	59
Jesus at the Globe Tavern	60
Memorial Day Contrarian	61
Join Rumi on the Grass	62
Memories on Nine-Eleven	63
Pentecost,* Hidden Harvest	65
Anxious Political Conflict	66
Remember My Name	67
Respect the Invisible	68
Revenge of the Oceans	69
Seeing Beyond: A. Wyeth and El Greco	71
Star Wars Salvation	72
The Holy Pause	73
The Muffled Voice	74
The Sacred Lives Quiet in the Ordinary	75
The Solace of Ambiguity	76
Voyager and the Way	77
Wake to the Wind	78
Toward Oneness	79
Which Jesus?	80
Will Work for Food	82

TOWARD GRACEFUL AGING   83

Aging Toward Reverence	84
Elder Prospecting	85
Emptiness at the Towers	86
Gifts from Stillness	87
Girl with Hula Hoop	88
Gym Zen	89
Here, Take This One	90
Late Love	91
Lessons from Elder Fatigue	92
Meditation at the Rescue Zoo	93
Migration of Matter and Spirit	94
Namaste	95
The Woman Who Was Free	97
(The Bentley Center for Adult Day Care, Athens, Georgia)	97
Wisdom of Gravity	98
Aging Toward Fewer Sunsets	100

POSTLUDE   101

Memorial Day—Procession of Ancestors	102

ACKNOWLEDGEMENTS   105

For My Family of Origin
As noted in the Prelude and Postlude

INTRODUCTION

I call this third volume of poems "The Hum of It All" to indicate a unifying process in my life. We are born into a world of dualisms. It's just the way things are from birth. We hear a limited range of sounds, but we know from science that we are unable to hear or experience so many more sounds, echoes of the Big Bang, that move through us unheard.

My Siamese cat Max purrs loudly on my chest to remind me of this bigger concert in the cosmic music hall. My choice of the alpha/omega symbol, linked with my family of origin, signals continuity. Many poems in this and earlier volumes point toward an evolving spirituality of insights from east and west. It's a way of echoing a motto from my Jesuit days of finding God in all things. But my view of God has changed. Now the divine is more beyond knowledge (agnostic), yet as close as my body and within wider nature as an all-pervasive mystery (pantheistic).

While unconstrained by the rules and theologies of religion, I've been pulled by them toward justice and charity. My path continues with recent surprises like cancer. This episode has been part of my journey from "sky" to earth religion with my brethren in garden, river, and forest.

I hope these poems depict important changes in my long life now nearing its end. I also hope that you enjoy the book.

"We shall not cease from exploration. And the end of all our exploring will be to arrive where we started and know the place for the first time." T. S. Eliot

PRELUDE

A Nightingale of the Temescal*
(Catherine Mangini Bianchi, 1905-1986)

"Write a poem for me today on my 112th birthday,"
she said, standing at the foot of my bed in a plain
1940s house dress, her head tilted to the side,
shrewd and self-deprecating.
Katie, my mother who loved me more than God,
a secret not grasped for a long time,
too many male distractions contending.

I grew up like her in an Italian immigrant family
in an Oakland compound before gentrification
built by her father Tony. He left rugged poverty
in the Ligurian mountain town of Fontanarossa
to start a horse and wagon garbage route
among his paisani and other refugees.

I've not forgotten the story of Nonna
holding you in your first year to watch
San Francisco burning across the bay.
I remember you, ma, sitting with Nonna
at our kitchen windows, reviewing
neighborhood vicissitudes, but not
having to worry about me walking to school.

And how many kids came home at lunch
to lamb chops and fresh sautéed peas
from Nonno's empty-lot gardens?

With a good high school education,
you taught me thousands of words
before turning me over to Sisters of the Holy
Names who eyed a priest-in-the-making.

We were poor but I didn't notice,
even when I got only a whistle
under the tree at Christmas.
Only much later did the great
photographers of the Depression
show me the dust-bowl Okies
trekking in hardship to California.

Your husband Gino was no piece of cake,
rather a piece of work with his angers
reverberating in that four room house.

Yet you had a way of stoking fires
and putting them out with the mantra
"Gino, don't get mad." What would
therapists have made of those scenes?
Gino had been through forty-four
months of the Great War before we
knew about PTSD, and the retreat
from Caporetto with horses shot
from under him and that bullet crease
on his head were more than after-dinner tales.
You defended him as a good provider,
not slight praise in a time of sadness.

You were proud of me in the Jesuits,
but later you loved women I brought
home, embracing them as daughters.
Mom, you may not have chosen the title,
yet seeing beyond rigid religion,
you were a humanist at heart,
making it easier for me to make mistakes,
and I hate to tell you, but you planted
seeds of my heresies.

Weren't you too hard on your brother
and my sainted uncle, Barba Johnny,
because in his loneliness and guilts,
he cursed certain clergy, housed
a multitude of stray cats, drank too much wine,
and didn't wash his clothes?
Perhaps along the way you glimpsed
some of his virtue, that special
man-child who confounded our pretensions.
It's revealing that his grave site
looks down on the rest of us.
Mom, with mature love, I see you
as a Nightingale of the Temescal,
bringing food to the homebound sick,
welcoming shunned blacks,
all the while offering
your shabby excuse for not going to church:
"Your father would get mad." O, you
were a clever one with that longsuffering look.

*Temescal: a district in north Oakland

BY THE OCONEE

Beauty and Depression

"Time is short. Hell is hot.
Jesus is coming. Like it or not."
    (Whitehall Baptist Church)

Many ignore this quaint message
in front of a nearby wooden church,
yet it echoes an ancient belief
and technique for religion-building,
the appeal to fear:
we sinners must be cowed
by threat of punishment.

And it works, given our millennial
terrors about present survival,
our longing to conquer death,
and avoid suffering on the other side.
It empowers pastors, improves tithes,
leads the educated to Pascal's Wager.

Scripture writers project this doctrine
into the heart of a wrathful God
who demands Jesus's death in retribution,
while we are left powerless, self-hating,
in need of clerical control.

A long history of politicians invokes the theme,
convincing the young to become martyrs
for kingdoms, nation states and caliphates.
It's at the core of flag-waving militarism.

Spiritual courage draws us to another vision
of embracing our basic divinity
and listening to mature saints who beckon
us toward freedom with alternate song:

"Time is short. Earth is beautiful.
The divine dwells everywhere.
Live with creative care."

An Inward Olympics

"Make peace with the universe...Resurrection will be now... every moment a new beauty." (Rumi)

My garden games at the birdfeeder
absorb me more than the big show in Rio
that's mostly out there: splendid bodies
running, jumping, swimming to defy
gravity at every turn.

I honor this symbol toward transnational
unity and its athletic prowess, sadly enmeshed
in doping and graft, loading debt
on the backs of the poor.

The Olympics portray a spirituality of separation,
pulling in dualist directions,
the Cartesian rift of mind and matter,
reality as parts outside of parts.

In my front yard I play a softer game
with the chickadee, tufted titmouse, goldfinch,
hummingbird and two crafty squirrels
who claim squatter's rights.

It's a nonviolent sport with rodents
outsmarting me time after time:
adjust the baffle up or down, trim back
a branch of hickory, move the stand
to higher ground…

I wave my arm cursing the groundlings,
urging them to share nectar and sunflower seed.

Suddenly it happens, a peaceable kingdom,

all seekers eating and drinking from the source
and under it, a quiet convergence
without gold medals and anthems.
In silent unity, spirit moves in and out,
And draws me smiling into the stream of now.

Are We God(s)?

"Standing on bare ground…a mean egotism vanishes.
I become a transparent eyeball; I am nothing; I see all;
The currents of the universal being circulate through me.
I am part and parcel of God." (Ralph Waldo Emerson)

I find it hard near my end to give up
the comforts of fear and armor,
to let it all fall to bare ground,
at least most of the time, swaddled
in fading tales of minor fame and beliefs,
even when I'm wrapped in the guise
of a modern bodhisattva.

Beggars and other humble folk are better at touching divinity than
theologians steeped in thick God-talk,
and preachers hollering or whispering at stained glass,
intoning the right way from this or that scripture,
as they carry down stone tablets every Sunday.

So hard for lofty ones to let go enough
to sense currents of universal being,
God everywhere and nowhere,
without demand to hold belief systems,
except away from mean ego toward loving community.

This pantheism defies pride
because it doesn't need it
to walk in paths of unknowing.

Lying back on a favorite sofa,
riveted by leafless trees
stark against a cold blue sky,
as the sun inches around them
in warm embrace through and through,

I get a glimpse of that place
between sound and silence.

Bringing Earth to Heaven

White mums, reddening dogwood
and a clearer view of the beckoning river
open the season of late aging
with queries about ending or not.

Life along the Oconee is a quiet preacher,
no afterlife sermons about bliss
or damnation,
no not-so-subtle demands on God
for endless awareness,
just beauty and resigned dying
as the vibrant coleus folds into sleep.

Religions have never liked such simplicity,
even today when love lyrics on ecology
hail from a Pope, shouts still ring
in the battle of heaven and hell.

Fear of death drives our cultures,
more now than when we buried
early kin with their stone tools.

Scripture writers were adept
at spinning tales of comfort and terror,
without challenge from Galileo and Darwin
to spoil our breakfasts and spawn so many
doubters and atheists.

Yet beauty along my driveway
has turned me into an agnostic pantheist.
I know less, but sense a penetrating oneness,
immersed in a cosmic divine,
closer than dolphins to their ocean
and flowers to their roots.

We are unfolding earth
now and forever.

Conversations with a Carolina Wren

"Poems spring up like the edge of driftwood
along the beach, wanting! They derive from a slow
and powerful root that we cannot see.
Stop the words now. Open the window
in the center of your chest,
and let the spirits fly in and out." (Rumi)

Let nature be my Ouija board,
my vast parlor for a séance,
as I press buttons to raise garage doors,
while Lady Wren speeds out of her nest
at the work bench to wait for me
on a nearby garden rail.

She's shy and bold with her piercing
call: "Teakettle, Teakettle,"
looking at me the whole time.
"Was I late this morning, Dear Friend?"
She dances on the metal, answers
with softer double "Teakettle."

"Will you vote for the Tea Party, Darling?"
Her head bobs this way and that,
then a melancholy "Teakettle,"
as she shoots off for breakfast,
leaving a white stain on the railing.
After all, she has squatted here for years,
it's the inevitability of influence.

Then up the driveway for the NYTimes,
that temple of Enlightenment,
with crows squawking and fussing overhead,
loud friends of the household who don't dive bomb me.
Watch out if you cross them with their long memories.

Am I slipping in my eighties?
It's one thing to seek deep purring
treatments from my muse and *curandero*
Siamese Max, like Rumi opening my chest,
but chatting with a freeloading wren?

It gets worse as I walk weakened hornets,
even roaches in tissue to the garden for a second chance.

Daddy Long Legs are easy to save, seeming
to bless me at the door and tip their hats.
Not so easy with three lost ladybugs
at my computer on their way to Canterbury.
Turn off the alarm, go into the cold in slippers.

Does this part time job come with aging,
keeper of insects and wandering birds?

Hawk and Dove at the River

"Yes, we'll gather at the river,
The beautiful, the beautiful river;
Gather with the saints at the river
That flows by the throne of God."
                (Robert Lowry, 1864)

Under birches on a bench at the Oconee,
I watch a peaceable hawk glide by,
hear an afternoon chorus of doves,
all living in us as gifts of mother earth,

who will sadly be forced to end our games
of mindless neglect a century hence
at seven degrees Fahrenheit
when dying heirs will curse us.

Then as an old guy, I doze off
to dream of a grand avian gathering
on this meadow to avert catastrophe
from our money-lust and joy of killing.

For long days they share this place
to explore our deep fears,
our lack of empathy.

Now I see them rise together
as a winged cloud
of hope and blessing.

Oak Leaves and a Puzzled Deer

Nature is powerful
but doesn't demand dominance.

Today I watched an oak leaf
float by still red, yellow and green,
drifting to its final rest,
waving its colors as it accepts
a career in mulch
to build its new arbor home.

The cycle is simple and complex,
as it dances from life to death to life.

We've become too smart for that
as streets run blood and terror.
We invent our absolute gods
who know what they want
from Crusaders to Jihadists.

Evolution outdid itself
along our shining paths
with only artists and other seers
to imagine roads we reject.

Then I saw a deer find her way
out of our fenced garden.
No need to call the marines,
surely she wasn't hungry enough
to eat it all, too busy
scoping out the puzzling maze.

I was glad to see her brown back
push through the front gate
to rejoin her herd with no
scheme to conquer the forest.

Red Hawk Teaches Meditation

Is my kitchen window a glimpse into the other side?
Earlier a rare red fox appeared on the path below
to lead me into dark conifers at the far edge.
Now it's the red-tinted chest of a hawk
sitting still as a Buddha,
soaking up divine rays
on a branch almost arm range,
like cat Tony behind me
fast asleep in a sun spot on the rug,
both in contact with the source.

Too unbiblical for Jehovah Witness Jack
who made room for me today at Starbucks
crowded with students possessed by computers
or texting in perpetual contact with the other.

No ordinary Witness, Jack, a major
fundraiser for slated Kingdom Halls,
who got a hint of religion when I said
his reward would be great in heaven
for offering me a place on the sofa.

Jack has studied all sixty-six
books of the Bible
and got it down cold,
though he wasn't sure
how the Dalai Lama might fare
after the final coming of Jesus.

I felt bad (well, not really)
about chiding him on theology,
but with no chance for the red hawk
to make it into Kingdom Halls,
I declined to give my email address…

This morning as I inched closer,
cell-phone camera poised,
the big bird looked at me without alarm,
seeming to say: silent, solitary, restful,
receptive, let it enter like sunlight,
no push, no stress.

Reluctant Nectar Seekers

I have tough mentors on aging,
hurry, I tell the hummingbird and finch,
come to my new feeder, hurry,
patience is not my strong suit, ask the ladies.

Not enough avian lore on Google,
I consult my inner scientist,
move the stand away from rosemary odor?
Less nectar and clean the classy container often,
for finches, loosen the niger seed with thin screwdriver?

Learn from a friend who attracts hundreds of hummers
to a cheap feeder set near a window
away from his koi pond,
check for predators like squirrels and killer crows,
move it again from thick shrubs with access for snakes.

Are they feeding by zip codes these days
or heading north to flee global warming?

Next I place it in the herb garden off the porch,
good visibility and escape routes,
they might like the scent of oregano or marjoram.

I sit behind a hedge to wait and meditate,
then flashes of yellow—butterflies?
No, three golden finches, so lovely
against the black seed.

Then a stray hummer hovers to get
a good look, pulls back, comes close
and lifts high to a tree. Don't expect
her back soon, as a scout must send
another to verify. Wrong nectar mix?
Still smells of ants? Do they consult the FDA?

Another day I refresh the water
in a nearby sundial, replace old nectar,
settle on a porch bench to rest
to await benevolence,
as it seems they can't be bought.

After a time the tremulous buzz
sweeps toward me in greeting
(they don't mind humans after all),
he darts iridescent green to the feeder
for another look, quick taste,
then shoots off to headquarters,
maybe the papers have arrived.

I'm moved toward Zen mind,
Zen breath,
watching
without demand.

Spirit Gift

"To turn, turn will be our delight,
Till by turning, turning we come 'round right."
    ("Simple Gifts," Elder Joseph, 1787, Shaker Community)

For years I noticed that chunk of rusted metal,
a very old auto part seeded here by the flooding
Oconee, possibly a throw-away from a Model T,
hanging forlorn and grimy from the white oak.

Then one day it dropped more or less at my feet,
but I hardly expected Moses's crib washed up
in the reeds or a piece of Athena's helmet
or Agamemnon's breastplate from the Trojan War.

This is not the land of magic realism, I say,
as I walk it to the recycle bin with ecological fervor.
Yet getting old slows me down enough to take
a second look at this strange work of nature's anvil.

Then yes, turn it this way and that until
it comes round right, letting the bird emerge,
rusted wings lifting skyward, eagle's head
soaring with the courage of many trials.

Listen to the Silence

"How then does one speak of God? Through silence. Then why do you speak in words? The Master laughed out loud. When I speak, my dear, listen to the silences." (One Minute Wisdom, Anthony de Mello)

Away from the roar of cutting firewood,
partly to tell myself I can still do it and
okayed by my overseer if I stay off the roof,

I settle on the old bench by the Oconee to
watch a silent movie at this
unlikely outdoor nickelodeon,
with light and dark clouds moving fast
against blue sky as the green river
carries its quiet waters across Georgia
into the Altamaha and on to the Atlantic.

It's one of those between-times when the
heat and stress of effort gives way to
a sudden shifting of gears in the universe.
Now the Buddhist prayer flags dance
in the wind as it whips young cedars
like pompoms at a game or parade.

Then in a flash he appears on the screen,
lovely red-tail hawk swooping all grace,
now slow, now quick riding the currents,
one eye on me – I swear it – the other on
his supper menu, all the while enjoying
this free ride on nature's carousel. Back
and back he circles down to a few yards,
as I wave to this avian Nureyev
pausing with wings full spread,

flashing his ballet style for unsung
bravos, encores and merited bouquets.

Now no noise in my breathing, just in and out,
with a virtual mantra: Buddha, Jesus, Red
Hawk, water, sky, trees, here, now, enough.

Talking with a Spider

Can you make friends with a spider?

A striking arachnid, yellow and black,
suspended at the edge of the herb garden
waits for free meals to tangle in her trap.

A writing spider, named for her squiggly
extensions above and below,
perhaps doing a memoir
about her life of pain and joy.

She seemed stable in her
well-woven place, then gone
just like that, by a careless cardinal
on a drunken romp.

Not so fast, as two days later she
rebuilds across the path to the front door,
and time for a tete-a-tete:
"Please, not there," as I carefully
lift her web and self back into the garden.

A few days later: "Is this better, Mr. Finicky?"
Ideal placement: too low for the soused bird,
but buffered by the strawberry pot and hedge.
To think we are the only smart ones.

This Sunday morning I greet her,
still as an acolyte before the altar,
a sermon on waiting in hope,
quiet resilience to face the unexpected.

The Oconee is Agitated

The Oconee is agitated today
after gulping down the storm,
as whitecaps break its surface
unhindered by whims of convention.

Don't sleep just yet, it cries, sit
still like Siddhartha before his
crossing to watch it all flood by,
chariot and charioteer, hangman
and victim, president, pope and pauper,
the abused cats and dogs of the world
with sad eyes borne on the fins of
fishes, hucksters of all manner
hawking paltry dreams of fortune,
the kind and unkind streaming by
to remind of supreme virtue, the just
and the unjust bobbing before the bar,
followed by peony and dogwood,
gracious beauties that bless our way,
loving women who bring their children
through crises and close our dying eyes.

Now the reflection of a barred owl skims
the water, moaning like a wounded
herald announcing my own return apace,
ashes to waves in the ocean of beginnings.

The Owl and the Mockingbird

I didn't expect to meet him
great gray-blue barred owl
walking the driveway as I
sought the New York Times.

I slowed as he flew to a sweet gum
limb ten feet above with curiosity
but not menaced by the rangy mammal
seen before on his property at the river.

Our reputation as tree-huggers is
spreading even among the insects.
Transfixed, I knew to go motionless,
even if he saw me blink and quit breathing.

So he sat for some time, no hooting,
no motion, no koan or death decree,
just master of this morning zendo,
calling to mindfulness and
reminding that not by newspaper alone....

That afternoon came the uncanny
mockingbird as I walked a tree-blessed
parking lot, his stage for wild song.
Don't tell me they don't notice
an audience even of one, mate or not.

I, too, used to dash from office to car,
deafened by cell phone mania rather than
listen to the stunning generosity of earth
art as he sang on from new to newer
tune without so much as taking a bow.

Such brethren breathe solace
in our world of ceaseless pain.

DEALING WITH CANCER

Cancer and Oneness

A cancer patient was someone else,
as other as a Kazakh or Maori,
an Arab or a Republican,
but not me in my splendid singularity.

Now it's me—I joined the club.

Yes and no, since I've only inched closer
to universality among all genetic kind—
the pigeons at the fountain, the elephants
in the Kalahari, the myrtle, magnolia
and fern gardened around me.

We are all one tribe blind to our oneness
until we let the great Tao live us
here now beyond comfortable borders,
sensing that mysterious force,
the substratum of all, linking us
with distant cells in far galaxies.

Wider than the call to specific faiths,
science in the concreteness of matter
shows ever flowing molecules
of cosmic DNA joining and parting
over eons down to surprise
sarcomas, hard signals of unity.

Beauty and Anxiety

"Let the beauty we love be what we do." (Rumi)

Many swords hang over elder heads—
will we outlive our minds,
succumb to falls and myriad diseases,
end up alone, unattended?
Anxiety grinds cold on hinges
of perception in a sleepless dark.

Yet with a new diagnosis of cancer,
the manageable kind, they say,
my religion has turned from the fright
of early years to the mirth
of agnostic pantheism,

removed from
the lessons of early mentors
who projected their fears of a
punishing God who seemed to hate
human cravings, a divine shaped
in our image clear and controllable,
not the surprising one of a mystic's unknown.

How did Persian Rumi grasp all this,
wandering the Anatolian sands, delighting
in food and wine, in memories of his beloved
Shams, becoming the flute notes Allah
played from the rooftops for dancing
dervishes and caravans from the East?
He had learned the hundred ways
to kneel and kiss the ground,
knowing he was one with it and could
relax into every molecule of the universe.

Compassion and Ransom

What a strange moment to have Manet's
The Luncheon on the Grass* come to mind,
with two lovely nude women and two dressed
dandies having lunch by a tree-covered stream.

After a good report from my doctor,
I stopped at a nearby McDonalds,
intrigued by a group of brain-injured
people with caregivers at a patio picnic.

The Impressionist gem reminds
of our love for the beautiful body
that Parisian patrons displayed,
not my view of brokenness outside.

Might a Van Gogh or a Goya
have risked the tragic scene
from their own sufferings,
able to capture its compassion?

That great virtue, if I gauged it right,
seemed to stream both ways
as in the gentle touch of a nurse
to lessen convulsive head movements.

I saw it again in the humor of feeding
French fries to the manually impaired.
The artists would surely have wept
and laughed, as I did inside the diner.

When the patients were led out,
hands joined, or on the shoulder ahead,
a hush fell over the noon crowd,
like *The Burghers of Calais*…**

wearing their nooses of ransom
against atrocities of the day.

*Edouard Manet, 1863
**Auguste Rodin, 1895

Crow's Voice at MD Anderson Cancer Hospital

He took me by surprise, shiny black-green crow
dropping into a dark granite fountain
just feet away, almost touchable.

"It's okay, Uncle, sit still, you don't bother."

Ravens seem to like me
as I watch their morning rituals on my driveway,
while they dive bomb the nasty, I'm told.

He evokes varied feelings in the hospital garden
when plunging deep, splashing, drinking,
content as a water-loving dolphin.

Does he announce a dreary nevermore
to a would-be poet or better song without
a crib sheet code-breaker?

The infinity flow over tomb-like stone
may tell my death, never far at eighty-five.
Still Lent, remember thou art dust,
and still hard to give up beautiful vistas
and loving eyes of earth.

Live with the daylight invader in fresh air
and cascading flow, adapt to its threats or
yield to the risks of the medical guild.

Yet a subtler message from the winged Mercury,
whatever choice, stay the moment,
your only life, here, now,
bathe with the bird,
emerge with Jesus in the Jordan,
hear the laughter of Lao Tsu
along streams in the hills of unknowing.

Martians and Earthlings

I'm not an adventurous guy,
first on the moon, third on Mars,
and I dislike the heroes of daring,
the Houdinis of space,
as dull as ramrod generals
wearing mountains of medals
for leading the naïve into slaughter.

I'd rather be a-bed in England
than follow Harry at Agincourt.

Mission to Mars plays down
militarism, highlights discovery,
a sugar pill to disguise the violence
spawned by fear, even the moon
is hubris enough as millions starve.

Why not accept a near century
on this beautiful planet as time enough
to tame the cruelty of our tribes
driven by utopian myths
of conquering death.
Better to embrace our lot as earthlings,
non-gods or godly enough.

I hear cries of anti-science Luddite,
but Martians may be the anti-intellectuals,
confusing knowledge with wisdom.
Limits energize nature—DNA is not
an afterthought, rather a plan for the embryo
of deer, dog and human.

Death is a boundary that can nurture peace
of soul and nation.

In the cancer waiting room at MD Anderson,
she tells her family story of the disease,
then in a rare, utterly believable tone:
"I'm happy on this day where I am."

The Chair Undergirds Civilization

The first carpenter placed the tripod outside the cave
to propel hunter-gather forebears toward new vistas,
and caravans stuffed it into spice bags on the Silk Road,
while Charles Darwin packed it into the Galapagos
for a closer look at evolving turtles and humans,
yes, the humble stool and its many kindnesses.

The mighty gilded it as throne of dominion,
see them carried aloft or resting on skull mounds
in the bleak cemetery of the everyday, these
generals of death and lords of gain.

Yet its humane aspect survives in the impulse to empathy,
as morning chitchat with Salvadorian Ana
about bathing after surgery in a slippery shower,
she, without fanfare or request found a plastic chair,
a minor gentleness upholding the tragic weight of life.

Here Comes Trouble

I'm not brave around medics
giving me the skinny on my illness,
but with age I'm bucking up.

They saved my life at MD Anderson
against sarcoma, not without humor
in the operating room and elsewhere,

sparked by the voice of cat Max purring
me into that dire chamber like a cantor,
after two false starts
for white-coat effect on blood pressure,

after my kindly surgeon and her team
came fully suited from scrubbing yet again,
determined not to turn me into Captain Ahab
with peg-leg, the old remedy, whale or no.

On the latest post-op, an elevator muse
inspired my stand-up comic: "Somebody here
is smoking pot." Loud laugh among cancer patients.

Not surprising that I was greeted in vital signs
with "Here comes trouble," from the lead nurse,
chuckles rising from nail-biting patients—
an invitation for me to hold forth—
Didn't Hippocrates teach you Do No Harm,
first rule of your saw-bones art?
Why push pressure up when I provide
normal daily numbers from my spiffy monitor?

Varian, My Linear Accelerator

Technology tricks me toward certainty
as I watch the great eye of the radiation
gantry, named Varian on his broad forehead,
rumble around for a point-blank shot
at the bull's-eye drawn on my thigh.

Two young women guide the robot,
then run away leaving me to his wiles
as he roams about firing three bursts,
then climbs over me like a bloodshot moon
with – I swear—an embarrassed wink,
for having missed by a smidgen.

Ours is an age of straight lines,
of precision strikes from afar, soundless
and sanitary, unlike iron balls
hurled at castle walls with bloody screams.

So we educate our young in neat rows
surrounded by computers that operate
in binary strictness to train students
to obey rigid rules for success
at the end of their lines.

Romance itself gives way to Techne
in our match-dot-coms dominated
by high school dictates of good looks
over diversity, laughter and surprise.

I promise Varian not to reveal our secret
to the single-minded in Frankenstein shops,
assuring that it's okay to stray,
to miss the mark now and then.

Outside the cancer center,
a stand of trunks and limbs
confirms my suspicion about straight lines,
pays homage to Einstein's curved space,

but mainly honors Siamese Max
who treats me in our reclining zendo,
squatting on my groin chakra, sending soft
vibes to caress the lonely tumor just below.

Belonging in Bishop's Park
Athens, Georgia

He sped by on a small red bike,
a ten-year-old black child
shouting "Are you saved?"
in a kindly tone, indifferent
to my Yes, this winged Mercury or Gabriel
left a message for soul and body,
as I finished a month of cancer radiation.

Sitting on my favorite bench with a
four-o'clock sun slanting in my eyes,
I admired the leafless, well-pruned trees
poised for rebirth without theological
niceties, while lichen glowed gray-green
on oak roots at my feet, all seeming to
be part of a bigger something very present.

Makes me wonder about religious
preachments on not belonging
until this or that confession, praying
this way or that with assorted rules,
or face a somber fate for infidelity.
Such fears spawn alienation
with its drive toward violence.

I touched the gnarled roots
that reached out to me in kinship
like the X-ray machine, sensing
a porous fraternity with welcome
rays of sunshine on my cool face,
the saving gift of inter-penetrating
unity against destructive urges.

CAT MAX MINISTRY

Cats for Reconciliation,

"The master chided his disciples when they strained themselves in spiritual endeavor. He proposed lighthearted seriousness or serious lightheartedness."
(Anthony de Mello, S.J., *"One Minute Wisdom"*)

Cats Max and Tony processed across the meditation loft
this morning as befits my smart kin assembling at a TV
for election returns and Judge Scalia's funeral.

They noticed the massive red mosaic over the apse
of Jesus cosmic ruler, a brand the Justice would admire
as his vision of church and court,
even if Ruth Bader Ginsburg might have misgivings.

Yet my felines themselves are evidence
of our slow mammal march toward reconciliation—
personal fear and tribal danger drove elder Max
for years to guard castle walls, wail warnings
and hurl back ladders of the stealthy brother.

So it was for us over millennia in the cave,
the hearth warming and feeding our dear ones,
while a graphic cousin sketched the hunt.
We needed the strong-bodied against mammoths,
marauders and threatening bands
with strange faces and puzzling words.

This history of fight-flight sank deep
into our DNA with political/religious
heretics to fear as in ISIS beheadings,
drone killings, suicide bombers,
and millions of refugees trudging
across borders, many to die at sea.

We cherish civilized breakthroughs,
but roots of the tragic traits persist
driven by lures of wealth and power.

Yet my cats, with serious and playful
clashes along the way, achieved
brotherhood and trans-species caring
in the spirit of great saints.

Death as Destiny not Defeat

*"Everything that has a beginning has an ending.
Make your peace with that and all will be well."*
(Jack Kornfield, Buddhist teacher)

Lent challenges me in old age
to a silence beyond religious rites,
beyond my sins and worries
about afterlife narratives,
or fears about returning to earth.

Francis Assisi felt a stillness,
lying on his back high above the town,
gazing at the sky over Umbria,
seeing the divine in every molecule
of the cosmos--sun, moon, stars,

even in dust returning to dust as sacred,
death as destiny within our temporal run.

Yet we want much more, devising
doctrines of eternal awareness that
become demands for the righteous
to reject agnostic unknowing.

Death becomes defeat
without the assurance of cross and resurrection,
rather than a sign of healing and peace.

If we accept the ashes of earth
as our unifying secret, we would stop
killing angels of diversity
in the name of purity, power and glory.

If we accept the ashes of earth
as our unifying secret, we can express
compassion for all creatures,
finding beauty in nature's vibrant now.

Here on another Ash Wednesday,
I feel cat Max purring on my lap,
see first hyacinths blooming,
and sense the world's renewal.
Take heart —our common resting place is in good hands.

Freedom Point

It's frightening to feel missed heartbeats
as the universe outraces our miniscule days.

Sometimes I sit by the Oconee River
to sense the freedom point for better aging,
surrounded by sounds of birds and rustling leaves,
as I watch for that in-between vision
of water moving while standing still,
like the flickering candle and its constant center.

We know movement from our first toe
in the stream or in the bathtub,
but life soon seeks happiness
rushing from one episode to the next,
one threat sneaking up behind another.

Yet the freedom point is not a still shot,
a selfie caught once and for all,
like snapping down the lid on joy in a jar,
nor a pledge against death.

It refuses confinement,
it's where we were and want to be,
owning not possessing,
loving not controlling, letting
the mockingbird fly and mock at will.

It's the space between the raising
and falling of the baton whenever we
let the music carry us unafraid
to a welcome place that surprises the soul
like the caressing purr of my old cat Max.

Let's not insist on staying there
by bribe or barter,
as the freedom point is too simple and wise.

Better to shuffle in and out
of the concert hall
or rest by the river
for a taste against fear.

Spiritual Infrastructures on Election Night

I'm too old to be affected like this:
sleep loss, night trips to toilet,
blood pressure up and bleary-eyed,
at the election shock of the Golden Narcissist.

No need to repeat blame on all sides,
not a time to build animosity and rage,
but how to create respectful listening
beyond the drive of fear and motive.

Start by easing my own despair,
yet feel it as long as it takes
to bridge-build from closed person
to closed group and slowly shape
spiritual infrastructure by reflective reverence.

That's the message of Siamese cat Max
who strode across the bed today purring bigly,
then got out the forbidden garage door,
just to prove he still could at sixteen,
softly laughing under my car.

The Hard and the Soft

"The soft and weak can overcome the hard and strong."
  (LaoTzu, *"Tao Te Ching"*)

Caring MD Anderson Hospital,
caring attached Rotary Hotel,
yet burdened with steel, stone, asphalt and traffic,
surrounded by medical high-rises so heavy,
pressing down on the soul, so heavy.

I'm grateful but saddened
that it has to be this way
and wonder about better sites.

Then "curandero" Siamese Max
approaches blue eyes wide, clearly thrilled
to find me on our meditation pillows,
as he leaps on my chest purring strong.

I missed you for the long time away—
let me face-mark the Tao book
to make it work with feline power—
where have you been, Dear Friend?

All projection, skeptics will say,
human emotions transferred to animals—
be scientific, it's all selfish instinct,
too much pious softness from Jesuit days.

Yet in first light it's bigger than Max
at this magic place along the Oconee,
only birdsong and green silence.

Would we could provide it for others,
while honoring this healing gift today.

The Hum of It All

Medieval nuns like Mechthild of Magdeburg
and Julian of Norwich kept cats
in their chilly anchoress cells
to ward off mice, they say,
but I think their felines cuddled them
at night in divine embrace, purring them
into contemplative union and sleep.

So I find it with Siamese Max,
a curmudgeonly sixteen who gives
his brother Tony the fish-eye,
yet the old guy with wonderful purr
is a religious whiz by ignoring
stale theology to plunge into core sound,
drawing me toward the source and sleep.

Lately I've heard that cosmic hum
from my hummingbirds hovering
with patience for my elderly pace
as I replace their bottle of nectar.
They carry the sound of all sounds
even when silent to our weak hearing.

Such meditation is not solipsism, withdrawal
into cozy corners, the world be damned.
It gives us time to slow down, slow walk,
slow eat with monk Thich Nhat Hanh,
to let things penetrate our subtle defenses.

It gives us time to feel deeply the sorrow
and suffering of child soldiers made to tie
bombs around their waists, of girls sold
into slavery, and of those starved
and maimed in continuous war.

It's all part of the greater hum.
I heard it again today in a chorus of cicadas.

The None Box

I do not check the None box
for religious affiliation,
too much like trying to look young,
but as I watch yellow leaves
swirl down and the white-capped
Oconee flood away drought,
I wonder about my aging spirit,
since it strayed from heaven to earth.

Mine is not a hard break from
tradition or community
or developing ethics—
rather an old man's fatigue
with turning Jesus into God
for the blessings of Constantine
and propaganda for church power
among hierarchs with their
long-proclaimed control
over afterlife, even over sex.

Many of them still talk
as if science and the Enlightenment
never happened.

My cat Max knows better—
how we are continuous with the rest,
because he senses death without denial.
I marveled at his care
for our standard poodle in her long decline.

I've come to whittling down
rigid beliefs to heart wood,
as I now mark the All box,
letting God-Tao be
deep within and around me,
a grateful agnostic pantheist.

Be Lamps Unto Yourselves

(Homage to Toni Packer, Zen teacher)

At the rim of death,
her husband cried out:
tell me what to do.
No doing, let it come unknowing,
it will sense what to do in kindness.

Figuring it out is great fun
and vital for the tribe.
We've been at it from Galileo
to Darwin to Hubble to Pluto.
Why this, why that—
such a thrill to see around corners,
talk with whales, sharks, chimps,
mothers-in-law and other unfathomables.

All great stuff, but it keeps us from
awaring,* from letting go me-stories,
me-attachments that cloud the path
through the woods of self-regard
to that clearing in the field
where we stand for a startled moment,
companions of everything,
without need to stake a claim,
or call for the assessor's eye—
this gold is what it is without me
and in me.

So practice closing down the ever wanting
me-machine churning from morn to night—
let now, just now, into the scramble that
drowns out stillness with room for everything,
without expected reward except for silence
that embraces all, a presence of the whole
from moment to moment, like the joy of being
with someone, something, that knows to listen.

Yet careful not to become too zen for Zen,
a subtle derangement of gloating in
enlightenment, again a me-story hidden
behind the quiet drama of meditation,

a tasty devil's brew of honorable deception,
a kabuki show of costume and movement.

Does cat Max, my zendo master, have to give
a harder whack or pour cold water over
my head of fantasies?

*awaring is Packer's word in her book, *The Silent Question*, for speaking of awareness, but with a more graphic intensity of immediate happenings.

REFLECTIONS ON RELIGION

Francis Dances America

With a combo of lyric and gesture,
he stops the Pope-mobile, lifts the five-year-old
in yellow dress from Nepal or Nicaragua
for a hug and kiss on his way to the Capitol—
which he would have done for the President's pet
had the water dog clutched the gift tee shirt
in his teeth, a clear preacher of *Laudato Si*.

He masters the sermon of touch,
embracing grieving families
at Ground Zero, and does improv
halting the Fiat on the tarmac
to hold the boy with cerebral palsy.

Like a deft pol, he kisses kids at random,
prays with diverse clergy,
invokes the Golden Rule to a squabbling
Congress toward the common good
of justice and service for the world poor.
His tiny car among limos
pulls us from false ego toward simplicity.

Applause in St. Patrick's surprises him
when he praises the Nuns on the Bus,
but does he see them still seated in the back?
He can't understand women as priests and popes,
too fearful a leap even for this dedicated dancer
and a clergy clinging to power.
But the Tao is patient even when he urges
having families on befuddled celibate seminarians.

Not always consistent, Francis moves deep
into big religion, the ancient planetary faith,
oddly going back toward the future
that won't surrender to magical creeds
except as temporary paths
that lead beyond.

General William Booth* and Senator Bernie Sanders Enter Heaven

Prologue: "You can't make it work,"
says my muse Max: "Socialism is not poetic,
and I've got better things to do."
He's a wonderful but stiff-necked cat,
yet we ancients can be stubborn.
Maybe if I start on the softer side—

Reminded of altar-boy days,
bell-ringing draws me
to the sacred red kettle
outside the local Kroger's
as I fish for coins to make a holy noise—
bills are better, but not dramatic.

As a long-time lefty,
I still feel a certain frisson
run up my spine enhanced
by the bearded smile and thanks
of General William Booth
promising to lead me into heaven,
"Have you been washed, Brother,
in the blood of the Lamb?"

Boomlay, boomlay, boomlay, boom,

from somewhere gentle drums intone,
while deaf customers glimpse
with admiration or disdain
for the showoff giver
and the white-bearded Booth.

Yet who can degrade the great
humanitarian who led
"vermin-eaten saints with mouldy breath
unwashed legions with the ways of Death"
to a better life even here?

Boomlay, boomlay, boomlay, boom.

From Trinity Church and Washington's statue,
marchers converge on Wall Street
with a thousand banjos and a thousand drums,

**Twanglay, twanglay, twanglay, twang,
Boomlay, boomlay, boomlay, boom.**

Inside they curse the distraction
from moneymaking,
yet they rush to windows
and sidewalks to watch
the strange parade.

The Senator's voice reverberates
in the canyons of greed:
"charity is good but justice better,
you cannot hoard the wealth of all.

Brothers and sisters, be washed
in the spirit of the great ones
who loved the light
of shared democracy
where avarice does not deprive
children of food, home and learning."

**Twanglay, twanglay, twanglay, twang.
Boomlay, boomlay, boomlay, boom.**

Onward to the edge of Battery Park,
they face Lady Liberty
who lifts her torch in blessing.

**Twanglay, twanglay, twanglay, twang.
Boomlay, boomlay, boomlay, boom.**

*General William Booth was founding first president
of the Salvation Army in 1865. I have drawn from
two poems by Vachel Lindsay, "General William
Booth Enters Heaven," and "Congo."

Inner Doors of Perception

"Seek without Seeking"
    (Zen master Wu-men)

Seeking pitches me ahead of myself
like hankering for the train's light
to hurry into the tunnel,
unaware of eleven Einsteins
on the platform ready to show me
the shortest way to Mars.

Before recall I was trained to seek
tomorrow's goals and public success,
tempered by Jesuit impulses toward good.

But let's not be hard on ordinary
planning, seeking nickels and dimes
to keep a roof over civilization,
bread on the table, art and science thriving,
nor deny the pleasure of forward thinking,
as magicians pull new rabbits from old hats.

Yet Wu-men wants us to relish the present
in its pain and uncertainty, to seek
without seeking, gripping patience enough

to wait for inner gates of perception
to part, as aging exposes
the limits of striving,
and opens doors from within,

to reveal a gift-bearer
with a welcoming, enigmatic smile.

Insecurity in Wee Hours

"Impermanence is our joyful situation." (Pema Chodron)

I'm happy about the summer storm,
the garden will love it, thunder
and lightning close to the house,
cats Max and Tony scurried under bed
as if they knew something was coming.

Power out, we hunt for flashlights
but batteries low. "Don't walk downstairs
barefoot," she says. Now computers
and phones out, while alarm system
goes berserk with incessant beeps
like a movie submarine plunging.

Two a.m. cell call to security company,
nice lady with commanding voice:
"go to basement mechanical area,
find the key, pull this plug, unscrew another,
try switches upstairs," then back down,
pinging goes off but returns
like a cruel ghost laughing in the wires.

Frustration all around, I retreat
to a lower bedroom, no sound,
only guilt assuaged by reason:
can't force her to come with me,
mama's boys stay with her.

"It's eight o'clock, O Great One."
Yes, the Verona blend will be our opiate.

This night reminds of our basic situation,
unstable in the best of times, as we ride
the ever-changing carousel of evolution,
every moment, every molecule altering
with pleasure and pain, while our egos
crave the illusion of stasis.

Master Jesus and Master Buddha summon
us inward toward confidence in the sacredness
of the world in its unpredictable sadness,
yet a joyful stage for compassion in turmoil.

Is Jesus God?

"Who do men say that I am?" (Mark 8:27)

Can I write an honest and reverent reply
to the query that shaped me since childhood?
Or does asking imply modern atheism?

After many centuries a yes response
seems to permeate things Christian—
great cathedrals and country churches
teach the doctrine, mosaics and stained glass
portray it, ritual creeds confirm it, painters,
sculptors, musicians, museums, theologians
and poets repeat it: the one and only true God
of the cosmos became man in Jesus to die
for sin and open the gates of heaven, that
final solace against death and basis
for the ruling power of hierarchs.

Questioning causes tremors under mitres
who insist on ancient imaginings as faith.
During Inquisitions denial could mean death—
Servetus in Calvin's Geneva,
Bruno in Rome's Campo dei Fiori.

No need to deny the wisdom and virtues
of Jesus, the Jewish teacher of Nazareth,
an inspiration for peace, justice
and love in face of pain and sorrow.

Yet ancients upheld the divinity
of emperors, kings and other heroes,
a stumbling block for many
in an age of evolution and cosmic science.

Darwin and the Hubble telescope pulled
the comforting rug from under certainties,
making it harder to view grand myths as facts.
Pantheist thinkers and mystics like
Eckhart, Spinoza, Emerson, Teilhard
point us toward union within Spirit now
in vast nature, respecting our unknowing.

Jesus at the Globe Tavern

Could it be him playing with gusto
in a circle of Irish musicians
doing their gig by the corner window?

I watch fascinated until he
tucks the fiddle under an arm,
rises and walks toward me.

"Jesus Christ! Can that be you?"
He hesitates. "Yes, we met near the Vatican
a few years ago at the Bar Blu."

He joins me for brown ale to say
how close Holy Week is
this year to St. Patrick's Day.

"Ah, Friend, with all the child abuse,
a dark time for Ireland's church—
plus Mid-East violence on the loose."

"Yes, Master, I see the tragic connection,
yet what about Easter,
any hope in the Resurrection?

"Well, religions reveled in mythic theology
when folk were ignorant of evolution
and turned imagination into history."

"Yet, Master Jesus, so much sin and separation,
how do we reconnect with salvation?"
He leans back, sips his beer,

and points toward the street. "See that homeless person
with her worldly possessions in a shopping cart?
Let's bring her warm nachos and a fiddled *chanson*."

Memorial Day Contrarian

(For Dan Berrigan and Muhammad Ali, war resisters)
"Obama Goes to Hiroshima."

Memorial Day makes me sad and angry
for the fallen on all sides,
more so for the hubris of leaders
who delude the young to kill and maim
in stupid wars for medals and ribbons,
for greater power and wealth of ideologues
who wallow in the safety of lies.

So easy for us to indulge flag-waving,
to cultivate enemy-making
and scream me-not-you dualisms.
Evolution formed this mania
on our fearful journey of survival—
so hard to move beyond tribe,
to kiss the other's face as one of ours,
so much easier to embrace bigotry
with vile stories about human and natural kin.

Paranoia impels us to inflate military budgets,
ignoring children without food and schooling.
Religions are supposed to correct this,
but they often turn into self-serving institutions,
tied in theological knots
and blind to their saints who preached
openness beyond our myopia,
dismissing sages of peace as naïve.

We have started honest talk about race,
but not about our militarism.
In times ahead an ironic hope
may open minds mired in violence
to view secular evolution and cosmology
as keys to loosen the divides of history,
and contemplate our common bond.

Join Rumi on the Grass

*"Out beyond ideas of wrongdoing and rightdoing,
there is a field. I'll meet you there."* *

Fear drives us to the strongman
      who steals our freedoms—
not to blame ourselves but to see it
      clear as a plain of poppies.

Dictators rule by threat, punishment
      and conjuring enemies
across the East from Sisi to Saud,
      from ISIS to Iran and Taliban.

For centuries western monarchs were no better,
      failing to heed inspiring saints,
they fostered fear and persecution,
      popes becoming vicars of a power God
in Jesus who wouldn't have recognized them.
      So do Ayatollahs take
Allah authority to themselves.

Let's look to an Islamic seer
      who stands for many others:
Rumi leads us from the halls
      of intimidation and false promise

to sit with him on a field of grass,
      transcending hostility to embrace
oneness with sustaining nature,
      engulfed in a spirit of beauty
ready to abound in diverse communities
      of our planetary family.

"Let the beauty we love be what we do." (Rumi*)

Memories on Nine-Eleven

Basement doorway, Nonno gives me a dime for a movie.
Ceiling lights go on. Manager tells soldiers
to return to barracks.

Walking home I wonder about attacking Pearl Harbor,
Pre-TV, I must await newspaper/newsreel
to see the Oklahoma explode in billows of fire and smoke.

I missed the draft but not the war,
the last "good one" blessed all around,
easy justification, no blood on our hands,
we're still the holy city on a hill,
eyes of the nations are upon us.

For naïve child at eleven,
all opponents are Satan,
firebomb, atom-bomb them,
nothing too violent for a God
forever on our side.

Soft knock on door, voice leans in
to seminar on American religion at
Union Theological. Kennedy killed.
Bob Handy pulls down Lincoln's
Second Inaugural "with malice toward none,"
we pray in James Chapel,
then sad walk down Broadway,
final cortege, riderless horse, John John salutes.

Too elated by Vatican II and MLK marching,
I now hear dark angels laughing
from empty benches along the street,
as death the brutal teacher
sends wild companions
to unhinge our golden doors.

Slow office hours at Emory
for Christian-Buddhist course—
someone has a TV, first plane crashed,
fireball in the tower, horror from afar,
death so sudden against crisp blue,

then the second hits, dead and dying
and caring rescuers rushing to die,
trapped in smoke and debris.

Osama cheered, but did Allah?
Technology abets our madness,
our meanness unleashed.

Fear undergirds these rites, fear of death,
of ego death, of the death of false desire.

We sit in a circle and weep.

Pentecost,* Hidden Harvest

All religions glimpse the spirit,
that soul within mind and thing
yet they box it in narrow confines
to enhance power and institution.

We honor religion's works of charity
even more when spread beyond brands,
yet doctrine becomes a devil that divides,
spills blood and bows to hierarchs.

Why would spirit not clap if kindness
be shown by Hindu or Christian, Jew
or Muslim, Buddhist, Jain or Sikh?

Or why would spirit be upset by our
feeble beliefs to describe the indescribable
in a cosmos rushing off at humbling speed?

Myth-making talent evolved much faster
than good sense about all this as we
fixed spirit in stone, rite, rank and dogma.

Let's call a long truce on such folly,
return to an earlier pentecostal harvest
sustaining all with bread and blessing.

*Pentecost is a major Christian festival of the Holy Spirit.

Anxious Political Conflict

They roared full tilt just over my head,
six crow fighters aimed at the owl's eye,
nature red in beak and claw, like it or not,
a cruel balance prevails between species.

With bigger brains, we've tempered
our violence in political battles over eons,
except where we continue to kill opponents
in dictatorial "democracies."

After this election, I'll still trust the good
sense of my fellows, and take my anxiety
to spiritual masters who counsel
alert unknowing and cosmic compassion.

I look forward to the mellow hooting
of the bard owls on a warm Spring evening,
and the raucous ravens at the river,
all voices of the world's oneness.

Remember My Name

In this mostly black McDonalds where I hover over
senior coffee to scribble poems, I wonder how many
slaves worked the land under me for cotton crops.

I mean specific people like the two hundred seventy-two
sold by Georgetown Jesuits in 1838 to Louisiana slavers.
So many are lost to memory.

Violence makes it into history,
like Nat Turner's revolt a few years
before Jesuits sold slaves to sustain the college.
The priests may have lacked Abolitionist fervor,
yet they kept exact accounts, maybe from baptismal
records to report conversions to Rome.

Jefferson's moral conviction all men created equal
ground against an economy based on slave labor.
Its brutal ways persist in habits of Jim Crow and voter denial.

The road to my house runs by cotton terraces of old,
now enhanced by pine and oak to cloak their shame.
These fields left an enduring brown stain on the Oconee
River, as if nature would not let us forget the forgotten.

I wonder how they travelled from Georgetown:
by road, in wagons, on foot or ship, a terrible
reminder for some of the Middle Passage,
as they worried about families divided, identities lost.

Respect the Invisible

Sometimes I feel God as close as my pores on a sweaty day,
or in a desert photo of kind folk feeding refugee children or
in Bach's "Sheep May Safely Graze" or in cat Max striding
up my napping torso to check if I am still breathing. (Odd to imagine him
giving artificial respiration even in his godly mode.)

Often the divine does not grip when I call up traditional
imaginings of old theologians frozen in creeds that we
recite like a worn shopping list with scant thought for reform. Such
doctrines turn into fossils strewn over the sands of time like the dead
remains of Ozymandias.

Spring is a better teacher of humility before the unseen
as the Lenten rose and lilac offer delicate flowers and
remind of hidden roots germinated eons ago
in the wild explosion of a thousand stars.

So let this season of new beginnings correct
our pride about religious knowing with unknowing.
Let the invisible dwell in its exceeding mystery
with only a welcome hint to enliven the heart.
Enough the dogwood and azalea to shout our limits.

Revenge of the Oceans

*"When man interferes with the Tao,
the sky becomes filthy,
the earth becomes depleted,
the equilibrium crumbles,
creatures become extinct."*
   ("Tao Te Ching")

I once thought education
would motivate change before catastrophe.
I'm much less sure.

Tell us the earth and sun will die in four billion years,
or that they began their union four billion years ago—
not a problem, too far, too far away.

Tell us the planet will be unlivable in two centuries,
we yawn, reach for a beer and watch football.
Scientists, novelists and movie-makers see Armageddon,
for most of us bored incomprehension reigns.

Short of nuclear disaster, we are unable
to cope with a dreadful tomorrow.
Our imaginations falter as they strive
to see and feel ahead, even to our offspring
unable to breathe in a few generations,
the very grandchildren of our grandchildren.

Too pessimistic? Or is optimism naïve?
The flaw may lodge in our genes—
For millennia we protected kin
in place or by moving.

Never have we coped with great cities
under water, millions displaced,
warring over food, shelter and land,
stalked by disease and starvation.
We are conditioned to think backward not ahead.

Even the tipping points only decades ahead
don't move us as our fossil fuel civilization
continues to promise a Cadillac in every garage,
personal meaning and success in accumulation—
forerunners of the abused oceans' revenge.

Hope may lie in our spiritual traditions
learning to love nature, plan wisely,
live simply.

"It would be difficult to overstate the threat of increasing human-made climate change, which we suggest threatens to bring about some of the greatest injustices in the history of the planet: of current adult generations to young people and future generations, and of people of the industrialized North to people of the South, as climate change is due mainly to emissions from nations at middle and high latitudes."

(James Hansen, Earth Institute, Columbia University)

Seeing Beyond: A. Wyeth and El Greco
(National Gallery, Wash., D.C.)

Wyeth's windows open on the Maine sea
and inward on missing actors whose
passions still drift through quiet glass,
and mottled white walls clutching secrets.

A breeze-lifted curtain acts like a diaphanous
veil revealing little, hinting more, a melancholy
tongue without utterance, yet promising tales,
sad and lovely, protected against the callous,

as it saves stories for those ready to embrace
the odd satisfaction of sincere voices.

So El Greco in another era pleases
and defies hierarchs, painting expected
lore, but stretched and distorted
toward the holiness of flesh,

all in blazing color to stun the eye
with inner pathos while satisfying
patron and inquisitor with a separate
heaven seeming to dominate from above,
while a strong-armed Christ whips temple defilers—
a wider mystery with common intensities.

Star Wars Salvation

A five-year-old in Darth Vader costume
holds a light/saber before a Christian altar,
summing up the theology of Force.

This recurrent savior fights armies of night,
sustains our violence against a world of threats
within and without.

An injection of arrogance
eases the pain of addiction to fear.

Star Wars is great fun
with music, narrative, visuals, sprinkled with romance,
as it repeats ancient themes
from Zoroaster's good and bad gods,
to dualisms of Paul and Augustine,
of Crusaders and ISIL Jihadists,
of righteous Neocons, all for the final victory
of our holy city over theirs.

An injection of arrogance
eases the pain of addiction to fear.

No need to walk inward with Jesus for forty days,
resisting the tempter toward ways of wisdom,
or with Buddha searching forest mentors
for the lotus of enlightenment,
or with Rumi whirling away pride
with dervishes in the desert,
chanting fuller union with earth.

Will the Vader child become a warrior, a carpet bomber,
or learn to speak and hear with respect,
to see through the eyes of others?

The Holy Pause

My anxiety dream kept showing the hands
stretching ahead with only nine minutes left to six,
urging action in lieu of cancer results pending.

It isn't nine minutes to anything,
just a now on the clock of aging
in the awareness of letting-go.

It's hard to calm our fears
of losing control of the uncontrollable
by fixing faith in changeless myths,
in hardened silos of religious history,
rather than count to ten with cosmic patience.

We call God and hierarchs to the rescue
with dogmatic claims that celebrate
outside salvation over death,
rather than seek inward for
a saving divine always present.

The most important theme in Buddhism
may be that pause in mindfulness meditation,
where we grasp—only idea, only feeling passing,

passing, to let the universe reset our inner clocks
to this loving moment
of empty fullness.

The Muffled Voice

It all comes down to the throat, that
passage of life, death and daring cry—
newspapers closed, reporters shot or
exiled to distant gulags for detested tales,
or dropped in the sea from army planes.

More images leap to mind: the twins in the
Tower garroted under King Richard,
a common practice among the mighty to
avoid contenders, stifle the threat of talk.

The bloody square and dungeon thrives
among us with gun and waterboard
to force a speech worse than silence,
that suppresses truth in its very name,
so neocons can thump their chests
and hawks continue to warmonger.

God's inquisitors know the game well
by edict, imprimatur and rack to block
heresy's mouth, to save souls from Satan.

We are more subtle than Putin with his
Pussy Riot girls and that young Korean
monster-in-training who apes master
Stalin with hidden camps where
protest dies along the barbwire fence.

The neck has its limits when squeezed,
even in lands of the free where corporate
greed kills the messenger by buying off
her radical cry while we wait for
the Fat Lady to sing Happy Days.

Still other muffled voices drum in
my ear like a tinnitus unrelenting
as I sense parental tears when a child
dies from umbilical strangling, the terrible
sorrow of a lifeline choking life.

The Sacred Lives Quiet in the Ordinary

*I found John LaFarge, S.J. sleeping peacefully
in death a few days after the killing of JFK in
November, 1963. We were part of the America
Magazine community in New York City.
He was in his cassock on the bed, his glasses
laid gently aside, the New York Times poised
tent-like over his feet. This priest champion of
the Negro and human rights was involved to the end.
His memoir is titled "The Manner is Ordinary."*

In 1540 the Jesuits started by revising
monastic ways without losing their core.
Ignatius said: our manner is ordinary—
immersed in the fabric of everyday life,
to find the divine in all things.

They failed in many ways
against the intense pull of past dualisms,
God up, humans down, nature just backdrop,
all swirling in cults of fear and punishment,
caught among religious/secular power-mongers.
Yet the ideal recurs now and then even in a pope.

Wonderful mind captivates us as we build
holy buildings, gestures, books and songs,
but the center of the wheel is empty,
an unknown void around which all revolves.

Smile on the lips is physical, less in the eyes,
birdsong is the physics of air to ear yet intent other.
The river rises and falls, a measured water,
its movement ever other—we never enter
the same place as it runs the range of feelings.
In extending waves, the meditation gong
resounds, touches the heart, stops at a door
of mystery between here and not here.

A gift of aging is to be unmoored
from severe convention,
to float and breathe toward
that unknown clime already
suffusing the cosmos
where we glimpse the ordinary as fullness.

The Solace of Ambiguity

Youth sheltered me from ambiguity
within a caring family,
stretching across the street
to Nonna, Nonno, Barba Johnny,
his chicken house chapel,
and the apricot tree by the well.

My school nuns, out of love of God,
sustained illusions of stability
in black and white burkas with hidden hair,
leading us in rites and rules toward salvation.

Many Jesuits, caught in Counter-Reformation
convictions, slipped around Darwin,
not telling me my fingers came from fish fins.
They delved into the western canon
without spilling its soup on their cassocks,
always submissive to the pontiff
and his episcopal acolytes of stasis.

Wider study of religion in freer air
brought me to mystic unknowing,
while fissures of doubt opened new paths.
Marriage failure brought experience
of new complexity baked into the cake.

Late aging summons me further
into agnostic pantheism where I hear
faint voices of a cosmic hymn
for day and night, for living and dying.

Creedal certainty matters much less
since I'm already in God engulfing
the mystery of nature and a vocation
toward compassion and justice

Voyager and the Way

"Not knowing is true knowledge...
The Master is her own physician.
She has healed herself of all knowing."
   (Tao Te Ching)

I wake up to framed drawings of Taoist sages
standing on a mystic mountain in China.

Today I saw them move on their way
to the fortieth NASA celebration
of Voyagers I and II: weird dream,
yet Carl Sagan, happy atheist,
savant of distant skies, might be pleased.

Voyager I is now eighteen billion miles from our sun,
racing on at thirty-eight thousand miles an hour
toward star Gliese, to arrive in 40,000 years.

If that doesn't humble us, try the new
Voyager III, to move even faster with a hand-held
Record containing libraries.

Voyagers confound the imagination
with their Golden Records, the size of iPhones,
giving portraits of earth culture
as gift to possible extraterrestrials.

Taoist sages have long taught the wisdom
of unknowing or not knowing too much,
over against the fixed arrogance
of philosophy, religion and politics
that urges us toward the violence of pride.

Just as these wise ones on my wall
stood against Confucian rigidities,

so today they challenge
our devastating certainties.

I will miss them from my bedroom,
but I'm willing to lend them to the best and brightest.

Wake to the Wind

"The morning wind spreads its fresh smell.
We must get up and take that in,
That wind that lets us live.
Breathe before it is gone." (Rumi)

I open the door to a concert of winds,
lifting leaves and branches in song and dance—
so aware of after days of breathless silence.

I take for granted this gift of life,
this abused child of the sun,
this patient companion of old age,
grateful as I climb hills and stairs.

From a porch bench, I watch it lift
cardinal and hummingbird to feeders,
disappointing squirrel and rabbit,
too heavy for their desires.

Wind teaches us to respect the future
unpredictable, as Spirit blows at will,
clearing ways for new hope.

In a predawn hour, I listen for different
breathings from two cats, a dear wife
and me, blending in motley chorus.

Toward Oneness

"Things derive their being and nature
by mutual dependence" (Nagarjuna, Buddhist Master)

I am an old man,
more aware of nature
when I fill the bird feeder.
I hear their communal chirps of thanks,
and calls to come and get it,
even manners as the birds take turns
from the shepherd hook stand.

We've become too separate
from our natural selves
by race, class, gender and other labels,
so it seems in this lovely Athens park
on my favorite bench,
late afternoon sunlight greening
grass, trees and rosemary.

Meister Eckhart and Nagarjuna,
spiritual forerunners of modern physics,
urge us to a deeper awareness of oneness,
every particle not a separate thing,
but a relationship right now
in my breathing and seeing,
a dancing texture of the cosmic quilt,
moving on its pathless paths,

near as the yellow butterflies
flitting around the bird feeder
from dahlia, to gaura, to phlox and lycoris,
enjoying their brief time without fear of death.

Which Jesus?

Stopping on the road to help a wounded stranger
or embracing the returned prodigal son
comprise core gestures of Jesus,
the migrant Jewish teacher from Galilee.

Jesus would never say he invented
the Golden Rule or universal love
or even "turn the other cheek."
Some hate to admit it, but the ethical Jew
or pagan Stoic would already be at home with it.

Religions at their best gather up
the gems of our evolving morality
as they appear along the Silk Roads.

But religious movements
must invent impressive tales
to compete in the market
of institution-building.

Who would be long satisfied
by a worldly life of loving neighbors,
when we might conquer roaring devils
through an executed God
to save from sin and fulfill
our fear-driven desire for afterlife?

Such strong myths need a champion
of vast secular power
like the divine Constantine
for a good chance of permanence.

Bishops inherited his empire
as princes of the church,
heirs of divine will to preach
Jesus Pantocrator etched in
ceilings of great cathedrals,
the lowly Jew become God of Gods.

The story has satisfied millions
for millennia with only recent
centuries of widespread dissent.

What if Jesus returned now
to this planet of violent oppression,
would he preach Hellfire and heavenly escape
or stories of Samaritans and Prodigals?

Will Work for Food

"How will the future reckon with this Man?
How answer his brute question in that hour
When whirlwinds of rebellion shake all shores?"
    ("The Man with the Hoe," Charles E. Markham)

I see them at intersections with forlorn dogs,
traumatized vets and other down-and-outers,
the underbelly of the world's richest.

I avert my gaze against embarrassment—
and sip lattes on my journey to salvation,
dreaming of gods in yachts, jets and McMansions.

But this one's worth a second look--
Good Lord, a true capitalist beggar
with lawn mower and flop-eared pup.

I hear fraudulent billionaires clapping,
since one day he too will finger a fortune
in pocket money to pay off jailers.

Then I notice a hoe at his feet, sign of
that terrible creature who one day will raise
his head toward a calamity of blood without mercy.

How might we answer that brute question,
our prisons already full of druggies, shoplifters
and jaywalkers, with no place for high-end crooks?

We could sentence them to time with tools of choice,
a hand-scribbled cardboard plea at freeway exits,
with a rescued canine to guide their souls.

TOWARD GRACEFUL AGING

Aging Toward Reverence

Aging slows me down
to cultivate reverence,
a core value of our long journey
to civility amid violence.

I'm still a learner in the art
of letting the other exist in me
with enough patient awareness
against my practiced urge
of racing to judgment.

Nature offers lessons
when that wild animal,
our Carolina wren,
calls out "teakettle, teakettle,"
before breakfast while I offer
a poor imitation as we sing
refrains like monks at matins.

Or in late afternoon I marvel
at the gentle respect of green gray lichen
clinging to its ironwood trunk,
both suffused in gold by the setting sun,
a mosaic of triple reverencing.

Or how I see many deer
on the side of my outskirt road
not as obstacles for auto damage,
but as part of me and I of them
with their side glances
of mutual acknowledgment.

To revere is to let in the pain of it all,
and its unfixable brokenness
as a cracked mirror of myself
without forcing a happy face,
caught between the world joyful and sad,

as I ask questions of our tragedies
to live into them with some redemption,
tracing a resurgent beauty in so much darkness.

Elder Prospecting

I sometimes feel like an old prospector
panning alone on a tributary
toward the great river of final return.

Many certainties have sifted through
the well-shaken mesh in conversations
with scholars and mystics who returned
to the forest to know less, to experience
and wonder more, while sitting on
the roots of trees in contemplative prayer.

Along this stream, I am less in control of things,
more drawn along with each gifted morn,
at ease with less doing in fuller solitude.

This is not a pursuit of shiny perfection
like the gold of self-betterment or great riches,
though I carry in my rucksack the Golden Rule,
a yen for justice and a candle for meditation
to curb old defects while honoring their power.

My mining is less about probing the unknown
than awaiting the unexpected to lift my soul
with empathy for the misery all around,
with the felt goodness all around.

Content then at end of day,
I assay my findings as wealth enough.

Emptiness at the Towers

Bright frozen void at ground zero 9/11

awaits the comforting cranes of our daring.

Does nature really abhor a vacuum

or does our gnawing fear of absence

drive architect and ironmonger?

Is it too hard for us orphans of the towers

to contemplate the nagging openness?

Is the great terror of that day

made worse by staring at emptiness

with neighbors falling from the sky as birds for death?

The terrible void shocks and challenges us

at the edge of life.

Gifts from Stillness

Across the porch, a stone Buddha smiles
at the yellow-black writing spider
who knows how to be still.

My running days are over, and fatigue
arrives as a vagabond to shut me down,
despite my offer of coffee and a power bar.

Slowed by my tiring visitor,
I sit on a gym bench to watch
the lovely young circle by,

and I'm surprised by spices from elsewhere,
stirred together in the stew pot of mind,
as if I had to close down to open up.

I write poems from this hodgepodge
parade of images, an un-beckoned
community: odd guests, from the spider,

to Walt Whitman to my unconscious,
to my cat Max who pops up unannounced,
to fragments of religion, all gifts of stillness.

Girl with Hula Hoop

Tall blond on park grass spinning her Hula Hoop,
shoulders to hips to ankles,
a balancing wonder on a late fall day,
like Shiva and the Blessed Mary
sitting on both sides of the Great One,
having fun hip-twirling the cosmic carousel
front to back, over and under, head to toe
while my black standard poodles chase
squirrels along the edges.

A broad sweep of places and faces
streams by from childhood
through later joys and pains, gaining a richer glimpse
from the hoop's last descent toward quiet grass
in grateful rest at the mystery of it all.

Strange to be sitting still on my favorite bench,
on this wide-beamed but deceptive earth,
sensing it move only by clock and calculus,
until I see the dropping sun isn't kidding.

Gym Zen

Rather than complain, I try to focus
on feeling in and out breath in my nostrils,
since X-ray plus diabetes fatigue won't quit,
I turn it into a Zen-lite med,
walk slow as an old turtle
around the indoor track at UGA,
just floating from site to sight,
hoping my monkeys of judgment
will stay in the trees.

Down below four courts of basket-ballers
flash in an out of vision,
one girl among them,
Asians grouped alone,
the shouts and big-ego dribblers,
(oops, a monkey loose.)

Cut off from command and control,
I circle like a tired drone
taking snap shots of repeated moves
to score for the hell of it, a kind of
muscular Zen from emptied minds.

Just now, just here with quick takes
of female shapes – short, wide, tall,
tied hair bouncing behind, some
even gorgeous by runway standards,
an overweight gray-hair chugs by
with desperate wheezing (away, monkey, away),
while young men run on behind iPhones
with the best looks they can muster for
this circulating harem, hardly noticing—
pure perfection —two amazing hunks,
biceps bulging from wife-beater tee shirts,
racing like the wind.

As mnemonics I count the laps in Italian
to the mile marker, sit on a bench, here, now
with the circus swirling, I contemplate
a round of tai chi in the dance studio with
kind dancers who make room for an
ancient Zen-ner, just here, just now,
with monkeys quiet.

Here, Take This One

Over half a century
I've kept a journal
to aid my hagiographer
tell the story of a
hubristic saint.

The composition books,
part of late-life triage,
circle me on the den floor,
testament to opaque tales
of failed marriages.

These pages swell
with searching, justification
and grief about wives
and therapists who tried
to shoe-horn me
toward less pain
on a foggy and embarrassing trek.

I may not have reconnected
with these depressing dénouements
now decades old, were it not for
the ink and dates on aging paper
that still clutch at the heart.

Mind dims what papyrus keeps fresh,
like finding logs of a long-sunken ship.

With weak radar in the spousal realm,
I needed special support beyond shrinks,
self-help and a parade of gurus.

Call it luck or miracle, but a former wife,
like the Oracle at Delphi, pronounced:
"Here, take this one."

Her insight was beyond my cunning,
as I taste this newer friendship,
a love less dramatic than peaceful
with humor and surface spats
between two who have learned
to write fresh pages together.

Late Love

*"Earth teach me to remember kindness
as dry fields weep in the rain."*
         (Ute prayer, American Indian)

Love word so used and abused
by preachers and crooners
from the Vatican to Old Blue Eyes,
from entombed Romeo and Juliet
to Nashville's factory of cheatin' hearts—
no literature, art or movies without it.

It sneaked up on me before I knew
from a caring mother and special uncle,
from teachers and friends, from years
in the Jesuits more in theory
than in celibate flesh.

Could this rescue animal be released near forty
into the wild, stumbling about with poor
radar re women, a delayed boot camp,
making his bed too fast, having to sleep in it?
The ladies were very good,
yet carried baggage that could not go
through security with mine.

If wisdom comes through pain,
I had quite a slog,
helped by peasant genes
that learned to make peace
with ordinary mind
and pulling up bootstraps.

Call it simple kindness:
twenty-five years with Peggy
pushing me to ponder deeper intimations—
yes, sexual attraction with highs and lows,
but a growing quiet pulse that survives
squabbles between the strong-minded,
something more subtle than early passion.

Lessons from Elder Fatigue

It may be other for aging others,
but in halcyon years, I never imagined
a new resident in breath and blood
commanding attention at whim,
pushing me aside for its dreary dance.

Fatigue is too common a word
for this intruder who I nudge away
with naps and sugar-free Starbucks,
hoping the lively mermaid,
crowned and ready to swim,
will lift me on her fins to a better place.
What a fun date not to be,
yet sweet in conjured memory.

I become tedious with complaints,
hardly the first to know deep
tiredness wandering in and out,
that makes doctors throw up
their hands and smile with a placebo here
and a pill there, a mystery beyond them,
since they haven't felt it yet—
buck up, old man, more to come.

Feeling weak, I sit under prayer flags
at the slow Oconee rolling green and silent,
indifferent seeming but not so---
we move too fast, missing fuller vistas,
still wanting to roar on unaware.

Less need for church-going now,
for building resume and legacy,
more desire for quiet being-with,
not pushing the river.

Let it surprise me,
pull me toward oneness
with birch trees, the flood plain,
my friendly wren and stillness—
more awake to being gathered into a greater all.

Meditation at the Rescue Zoo

Bear Hollow Zoo, Athens, Georgia

The barred owl with one good eye sits in the doorway of his rustic condo
like a Buddha to tell me
I have become a rescue animal in late life.

I want to say no, look—I still write poems,
but he's right as gates close
along old frontiers with fewer entry points.

Don't get maudlin with self-pity, he says,
seek peace with the white-tail deer smooching
in the grass, make friends of fatigue,
welcome love enough,
and nap in mid-afternoon with the alligators.

Toddlers leap at finally spotting him,
"What's that, Mommy?"
pointing at the striped bird,

who lets the world approach as it will
teaching the wisdom of vulnerability
to enhance wounded life in the future.

I watch two orphaned black bears
celebrate their sixth birthday
with peanuts and cupcakes,

dance with special dexterity,
as they open curious gifts
to give a wordless homily
about cross-species care, their
human staff enjoying the show.

Would that the UN might create
zoo schools where diplomats serve two months
as hands-on custodians before they sit down
at the great tables in Geneva
to empathize with unrescued peoples.

Migration of Matter and Spirit

Right after my mother Katie died thirty years ago,
I felt the presence of monarch butterflies
around a bench in the garden,
a premonition beyond knowing,
carrying a consoling presence.

Again yesterday I saw them feeding on flowers
as they returned north from those special hills
and trees in Mexico on their annual
pilgrimage toward warmth and new life.

The Canada geese are back
honking their way up the Oconee River,
a special song of their migrating cycle,
lovely as the hooting of local owls.

We like to think we are better
with spectacular brains beyond
genetic compulsion as we plunge forward
to devise splendid cities and science.
We are entrepreneurs of tomorrow.

Yet aging brings on enough stillness
to let deeper truths rise, that we are
migrants of spirit and genes.

Mother Katie is more than a photo on my desk.
She carried forward generations of Genovese
from the high country of Liguria, perhaps with traces
of medieval Saracens who settled
nearby in the tenth century—

she goes back thousands of generations
before Sumer, back to that celebrated
ancestor we like to call Eve.

Even this sweep is a cribbed history,
as my mother and I descend from ocean
creatures who became land and air migrants.
I need look no further than my morning mirror
to find the forward migration of spirited matter.

Namaste

Too young to know better,
I presumed utopia
around the bend,
naïve about death
strolling well behind,
surely my cohort
would keep him at bay.

Now we walk side by side,
my pace slowed, his steady—

no need for him to hurry as he goes about
making many mind-sick
and soul-sick
with torments of everyday consciousness.

Euripides, early shrink-playwright,
dramatized the bakkhai prescribing
wine as remedy for these blues.
Now it's heroin and more.

And where would Shakespeare be
without Hamlet's misery,
or today's best writers without such anxieties?

Now older I experience
this heartbeat of history,
driving us to fame and gain
to dull the panic of the terrified.

Many followers of religions
take comfort in promises of
afterlife, described by preachers and holy books.

Once a believer in this reward,
I've turned unknowing,
to find meaning
in here and now gestures
to mitigate such built-in suffering,
without getting mad at God
for reneging on heaven

or any need to strike
Pascal's wager.

An eastern prayer,
greeting and farewell,
Namaste, invites me back
into body and earth,
with bows and hand movements
to foster community
on a common path.

Namaste—may the spirit in me
honor the soul in you—with thanks
for the journey and few regrets.

The Woman Who Was Free
(The Bentley Center for Adult Day Care, Athens, Georgia)

Three of us bring this month's poems, singing and music
about freedom and the Fourth with fingers crossed.

Silly of the poet to deny liberty's many sides—
the armies that march for it, the justified bombs
that promise it, the hard work of liberating
ourselves from its cultural enslavement.

On this sixty-fifth anniversary of friendship
between Ginsberg and Ferlinghetti,
there is still so much to howl about,
that life-preserving bardic cry
to unravel pretension with its endless desires.

In red, white and blue décor, we read old
poems and sing known songs to spark
dim memories, inviting folk to join
with voice, hand gestures, even dance.

Yet my joy turns sad sensing my own decline
mirrored in theirs, feelings so easily
dismissed in earlier strength.

In parting, I ask about personal
moments of freedom over lifetimes,
as a final response takes me by surprise.

"I feel most free right now," she says,
smiling through disabilities.
Did all the clocks in the universe hiccup
for a nanosecond?

What strange mystery this. Was it Jesus
preaching the inner kingdom, or Rumi
whirling happy with dervishes
on the sands of Anatolia, or Buddha
smiling at the uplifted lotus flower?
We came as cheerful choreographers,
confident in our gracious schemes,
when the afflicted woman cut to the heart.

Wisdom of Gravity

(*Il faut finir bien.* —Teilhard de Chardin)

To appreciate gravity is a gift of aging,
to embrace that force pulling from the womb,
as we stretch upward on wings of Icarus.

We search the sky with space ships,
reach up with personal projects,
seek and serve worthy goals,
ever excelsior, never looking down.

Our weak egos demand such motion
lest we lean our faces too soon
against the side of the crib and die.

In my ninth decade, I feel the tug
as recurring fatigue
that I try to befriend as he walks
toward me with a soft smile,
tip of the hat, even admiration
to help me finish well—

a mile on the indoor track,
with youthful deniers, lost in iPhones,
running ahead with kindly looks,
Are you still alive?

Mr. Gravity will win the race—
it's happened too many times
to bank on cryogenics or new quarters
in the salvific air of Alpha Centauri.

Yet the slow fade of aging has moments
of lovely decline with a brief to-do list,
no bosses to please, feeling closer to the owl,
the hummingbird, and singing wren
who greets me at first light in our duet of calls.

In this election season, I watch
the great ones soar over the country
with breathless pledges for
our welfare and their legacies.

Not much younger than myself,
they don't notice Mr. Gravity
in a corner of a cheering rally,
waving a sign, about to ask an autograph.

Am I secretly jealous of the famous
who keep defying gravity? Perhaps so,
but there's something to be said
for heeding its pull in late life,

as a silent call to embrace each moment,
aware and caring.

Aging Toward Fewer Sunsets

Much about aging is waning odds on a roll of dice,
things they don't ask you to lift,
a few more bicycle rides avoiding the hills,
and a recurrent fatigue that throws a sudden pall.

Easy to get maudlin about it and sit sad
on the grumbler's bench, or fake bonhomie
with thumping bravados of not me, not me,
embracing the lame heroics of futile dreams.

I read old journals as a museum of myself,
albums of smiles, joys, struggles and pain,
a kind of vibrant wrestling with the unfinished,
not knowing how it will turn out.

As the flooded river moves slow against purple-gold
clouds repainting themselves at the dimming of day,
I circle the stone labyrinth behind my house,
an invitation to heed beloved ashes at the center.

POSTLUDE

Memorial Day—Procession of Ancestors
Memorial Day, 2015

We've become too secular for them,
not even a limbo or purgatory
for these poor ghosts

unless you sit on the wooden stairs
of your growing-up house
and stare at the corner mom and pop
grocery, long since a cheap nail parlor,

I mean look hard—
I mean gaze until your eye lids hurt
or a passer-by fingers her iPhone,
worried you need First Responders.

Take a chance on looking crazy,
your long hidden state as an academic,
now beyond promotion
and nearing that intermediate realm,
that middle zone honored in Nigeria
and Tibet and other so-called backward
countries short on fast food, running water,
debutants, and the NFL.

Look, look, be amazed, right there
at the blue mailbox on 42nd and Market,
see them coming around the store—

Nonno leads in faded black jeans
and galluses, pushing my old bicycle,
ready to tap the barrel
and wag his kindly mustache
at nonna's list of woes.

Then he winks at me, calls "Jewging,"
ready to hand over a dime for the movies.

She in long, heavy cotton skirt, a pillar
of perseverance, pitchfork over shoulder
to loosen soil between tomato plants
and some lucky snapdragons,

second raters in a Ligurian garden—
you have to eat: *primum est esse*.
She looks my way, lifts her head,
signal to come/listen to the Italian newspaper.

Then Katie in housewife dress,
pushing younger son in a stroller
and holding my hand,
back from counseling or consoling a
neighborhood grievance to start supper
and pull down the wall ironing board.

Gino comes around in welder outfit,
car-pooling from the Vallejo navy yard,
black metal lunch box in hand—
is he angry or just tired or both?
We hold our breath, but depend on
his stability under nightly dramas,
hoping she doesn't ask if he's mad.

Finally, in paint-stained white coveralls,
Barba Johnny, a found radio speaker under one arm
and a stray cat nestled in the other,
a new refugee for his feline encampment—
he calls my earliest nick name: "Putiti, Putiti."

So flawed saints come back to their compound
unseen by today's tenants, only by the intent eye.

So will minor celebrity be short-lived,
yet valued for its kindness and caring.

ACKNOWLEDGEMENTS

I am very grateful to poet and engineer Bob Ambrose for his wonderful and kindly help with IT skills and other talents to shape this book. I am also very thankful to poet, photographer and cartoonist, David Noah for photos front and back as well as his cat Max drawings through the book. And I acknowledge Siamese cat Max, my dear and curmudgeonly muse, who inspires many poems.

www.ingramcontent.com/pod-product-compliance
Lightning Source LLC
Chambersburg PA
CBHW050203130526
44591CB00034B/2027